FORGIVENESS

Healing the Harbored Hurts of Your Heart

Bill Elliff

with Tim Grissom

Forgiveness

Healing the Harbored Hurts of Your Heart

By Bill Elliff

Eighth printing March 2011
Printed in the United States of America

Published by TruthInk Publications
6600 Crystal Hill Road
North Little Rock, Arkansas 72218

Design by Keith Runkle

ISBN: 978-0-615-40308-3

I cannot imagine a more ideal childhood than my own. A godly, pastor-father led our home with strength and purpose. We believed our dad had the greatest, most important job in the world; and we often saw around us the evidence of changed lives resulting from his ministry. God so prospered my father's hand that the churches he pastored experienced some of their greatest days during his tenure.

Dad's life challenged his three sons and one daughter. He lived on purpose—to bring men and women, boys and girls to Christ—and he passed this desire to us. When God called each son into the preaching ministry and the daughter to be a preacher's wife, we saw this calling as a privilege, not a duty, and responded with joy and gratitude.

And my mother filled our home with light. Unshakable faith, eternal optimism, and simple joy flowed freely from her heart and wrapped our home in a warm blanket of security. She gave us the legacy of unconditional love.

As a child, I assumed every home was like mine. We had no overwhelming difficulties nor great complications. Even in my early years of adulthood, when I attended seminary and began my full-time ministry,

I often wondered why our family had been touched by so little pain.

But that soon changed.

My father had been so used of God that he was asked to give oversight and help to large groups of churches within our denomination. By the time he reached the mandatory retirement age, Dad had accomplished all of his goals and more. However, over a period of several months he experienced a series of disappointments, followed by a season of depression and despair. This vulnerable time opened a window of temptation.

My father then faced and failed the greatest test of his life. He fell into an immoral relationship.

Through the providence of God we became aware of what was happening. I was shocked to even consider that my father had fallen into such sin, but the evidence continued to mount. Finally, my brothers, sister, and I did something we never dreamed would be necessary. Together we went, unannounced, to my parents' home where we confronted our father. It was our great love and our desire to see him rescued that compelled us to take such a difficult step.

Sin always brings turmoil, and our family was no exception. We boarded a roller-coaster ride of uncertainty and upheaval that lasted for over two years. Dad went up and down, and back and forth. One day we would think his heart was returning to his family and his God, only to be disappointed. There was a time when he left home, then returned several days later. I vividly recall pleading and reasoning with my father as we talked in his workshop, trying desperately to pull him out of this awful confusion.

We all prayed, and fasted, and wept . . . and HURT.

Much of my theology was shaken. Everything I had ever known was called into question, for the one from whom I had learned these convictions was falling.

"Why would God allow this to happen?" I questioned. "Weren't we trying, as a family, to serve Him? Why wouldn't God answer our prayers and answer them now? How could a loving God allow his children to suffer so? Is God always true to His promises?"

One day, upon returning home from an errand, my mother found a simple, sad note on the kitchen table. Dad was gone.

In the subsequent days my father initiated a divorce and married someone else. Dad had walked away from our lives.

It is still amazing to me that the one who hurt the most outdistanced all the rest in her response. But then, that's the kind of woman Mother was. The breadth of her forgiveness sprang from the depth of a relationship long-developed with the Lord. She had her questions, fears, doubts, and pain; but she clung to the Lord with amazing faith.

It was from my mother—through her words and life—that I learned the power of forgiveness. At every turn (as you'll read later), she chose to handle her hurt God's way.

But what if she had resisted? What would have happened if Mother had chosen to harbor her hurt? What if she had taken the well-worn path on which our emotions normally run? My mother would have been no exception; she would have suffered the devastation of harbored hurt.

Have you ever been hurt? Perhaps by:

- parents who didn't offer the love and affection you felt you needed
- a child who disappointed you, or rebelled against your authority
- the break-up of a love relationship
- a work colleague who betrayed you
- a teacher who embarrassed you in front of your classmates
- an oversensitive or quarrelsome neighbor
- a friend who stabbed you in the back
- a gossip who damaged your reputation

Or perhaps it was not a person, but some circumstance or event that brought great pain into your life:

- a tragic accident
- a financial crisis
- the death of a loved one
- being overlooked for a promotion
- a physical deformity or disability
- losing your job

… or other unforeseen, unexpected circumstances over which you had no control. Even though there was no one to blame, no person to point to as the cause, you hurt just the same.

The truth is, as long as you have breath in your body, you're at risk. If you haven't been hurt yet, just keep living! Some hurt is out there, tagged with your name and address.

The greater question is not, "Have you been hurt?" but …

How do you handle the hurts of your heart?

Although your reactions may manifest themselves in a number of ways—from skepticism and suspicion, to anger and revenge, to withdrawal and depression—there really are only two available options in dealing with your hurt.

You can either …

> *harbor the hurt, or*
> *heal the hurt God's way.*

When we are hurt, there is often an initial moment when we are so stunned we simply don't know what to do or say. At that instant, our emotions may run the gamut. We may collapse in grief, cry out in pain, or seek temporary solitude away from everything and everyone. Be assured that God understands our initial reactions just as a loving father does when his child is injured. This is not to imply that God would ever turn a blind eye to sin, but He is well acquainted with our frailty and listens with compassion to the cry of our heart (Heb. 4:14-16).

In time, however, and as soon as possible, the hurt must be faced and dealt with productively. Pain may linger—some pain is even useful—but harbored hurt has dangerous effects and must be released.

Hurt can be like an enemy warship deceitfully sailing under a friendly flag. If we offer it safe passage and permit it to enter our harbor, we unwittingly welcome enemy troops to our shores. When we finally awaken to the truth, we find that we are under siege.

Too often we do harbor our hurt. Not quite certain what to do, we tuck hurt away in our souls … unaware that it has a life of its own.

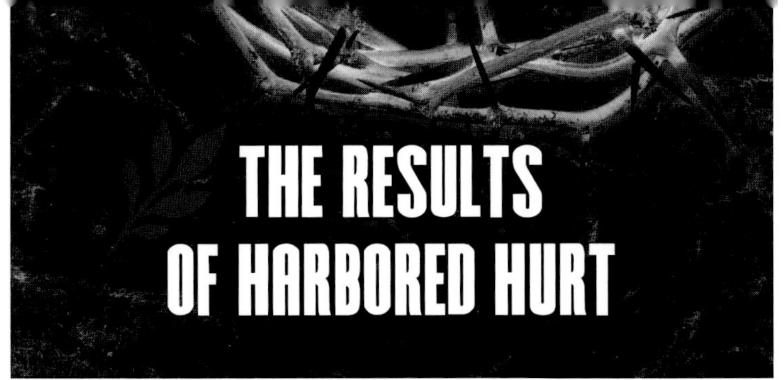

THE RESULTS OF HARBORED HURT

Stockpiling hurts in our heart brings about the development of bitterness. Like a poisonous vine, bitterness can wrap itself around our emotions, penetrate our thoughts, and choke the life from our soul. Bitterness robs us of joy and peace. It hijacks us; taking us places we never wanted to go, doing things we never wanted to do, and making us people we never wanted to be.

Bitterness is subtle. I've rarely met a bitter man who realized his condition. No one wants to think of himself in this way. The very word "bitter" sounds appalling to our ears. It's a label none of us want; yet by my own experience, I can tell you that many more of us are bitter than care to admit it. Passing through a bitter season in my life, I was oblivious to my condition. All the while I counseled people who were bitter, and even preached about bitterness. I could recognize it in others, but not in myself.

Sometimes bitterness is misdiagnosed because there has been no massive tragedy or great pain. We erroneously think that only those who have been gravely hurt become bitter. In reality, the smallest particle of harbored hurt carries deadly potency, just as one cancer cell has the potential to fell the strongest of men. Would you be content to do nothing if you knew that just a few cancer cells had been found in your body? Are you also willing to look with indifference to the hurts of your heart? If Satan can keep you blinded to the presence of bitterness, however small and harmless it may seem, he has an open door.

Would you, before the Lord, keep a humble heart and mind as you read on? If you have been hurt at some point in your life, would you be honest enough to pause right now and sincerely pray …

Lord, if there is any bitterness in my heart, would you reveal it to me today?

Although we often cannot see bitterness in ourselves, its effects disclose its presence to others. The writer of Hebrews uncovers for us three of the most damaging results of bitterness:

> *See to it that no one comes short of the grace of God; that no root of bitterness springing up causes trouble, and by it many be defiled; … (Hebrews 12:15)*

BITTERNESS ALWAYS SPRINGS UP

Even if we are aware of some hurt brewing inside us and intentionally try to hold it in check, it will find a way to seep through our soul. Hurts have a life of their own; and true to their nature, will always break through the surface and manifest themselves in some form.

Several years ago a friend volunteered to mow my lawn while I was out of town. Before leaving, I forgot to mention to him that I had been nurturing a tiny sapling in our yard. When I returned, I discovered that he had accidentally stripped its tender bark with a power trimmer. The sapling appeared to be so badly damaged that I simply mowed it down. However, throughout the rest of the summer small sprouts continued to break through the soil. Even though I had cut away everything I could see above the ground, there was still life in its root system. The sapling kept trying to grow.

When hurts are not dealt with God's way, bitterness roots itself in our soul. Like the sapling that refused to die, bitterness will continually spring up.

BITTERNESS ALWAYS CAUSES TROUBLE

Have you ever eaten a persimmon? It's a bitter, bitter fruit. Do you know where the persimmon fruit comes from? A persimmon tree. And do you know where a persimmon tree gets its life? From a persimmon root! Go to the farthest end of the longest limb on a persimmon tree, and do you know what kind of fruit you will find? You may hope for sweet cherries, but you'll only find bitter persimmons. Bitter roots always bear bitter fruits.

In the same way, a bitter root in your heart will manifest itself in troublesome attitudes, such as depression and despair, anger and resentment, or fear and worry. Your reactions may become typified by criticism, slander, gossip, sulking, retaliation, or other caustic behavior.

Nobody likes to get hurt, especially for the second time. If a dog were to bite you, you'd probably do your best to never meet that dog again! After being bitten by a painful experience, we sometimes develop strategies and adjust our behavior, thinking this will protect us from future hurt. Repeated often enough, this habitual behavior ingrains itself in our character. It becomes who we are and what we do.

Are you the type of person who has to control every situation? Do you frequently lash out in anger? Are you manipulative? Have you become so oversensitive that others feel they must "walk on eggshells" whenever they approach you? Do you keep up a facade so others can't really get close to you, or know who you really are?

All these behaviors, and others, are methods we sometimes develop to shield ourselves from further hurt. As you can see, they are brimming with destructive consequences. The very strategies we use to avoid hurt only multiply the pain to ourselves and others.

When we harbor hurt—perhaps for years—it has the capacity to drive our every action, affect our every decision, and sour our every relationship. It will always make its presence known. And we'll regret it.

BITTERNESS ALWAYS DEFILES MANY

Bitterness cannot be quarantined. Like an epidemic, it spreads. One bitter person has the capacity to infect an entire classroom, corporation, or congregation. Hurting people hurt people.

Entire families can be poisoned. Harbored hurts and bitterness can literally be passed from one generation to the next (Num. 14:18). I once knew a very bitter man. Upon investigation I discovered a wound in his heart that was still festering after 40+ years. His life manifested all the fruit of a bitter root. It did not surprise me when I witnessed his son and grandson also carrying a bitter spirit. Could there be any harsher judgment against the sin of bitterness than being guilty of infecting the ones we love the most?

Diseases such as AIDS and hepatitis are so ominous because they're so highly contagious. Bitterness is equally vicious. It is never satisfied with just one victim.

Bitterness will always spring up, always cause trouble, and always defile many. You may think you can hold on to your hurts and not be adversely affected, but you are wrong. You cannot fathom how a root of bitterness will influence your thoughts and decisions, and your attitudes and actions. Much of your life will be driven by bitterness if you permit it to develop in your heart.

- Is it really worth holding on to your hurts?
- Is the pain worth the price?
- How much of your life are you willing to exchange simply to harbor your hurt?
- Who among your friends and loved ones are you willing to risk defiling with the poison of your bitterness?

THE REMEDY

Having faced the options available to you—harbor your hurt, or heal it God's way—you may have already decided to do nothing. Hopefully though, you have realized the potential fallout from that response and are ready to pursue God's remedy.

So, where do you go from here? How do you overcome the hurts you have been harboring? What must you do to alleviate your bitterness and neutralize the acidic effects it has left in your soul?

God has a wonderful plan for complete freedom and healing. You will be amazed to discover (if you will fully follow His leadership) that God can take you beyond the mere removal of bitterness into the realm of genuine thanksgiving. He can even give "beauty for ashes" by using the pains of your past as a springboard of ministry for the future. Not only can the hurts be overcome, they can be a means of ministering to others for their good and God's glory. Only God could do something like that!

The following principles can transform your life as they form God's path to bring deliverance and usefulness, even in the midst of great pain. You cannot take these steps on your own. They are only possible through God's enabling grace which He gladly gives as we humbly cry out to Him. Ask Him right now for grace to understand and grace to obey.

1. RECOGNIZE AND ADMIT YOUR OWN SIN

Admit my sin?! Don't you know it was the other person who sinned against me? If anyone needs to admit their sin, it's them!"

You're right, they do. However, your healing does not depend on their response. You cannot change the offensive person or the hurtful situation; but you can, by the grace of God, change your attitude. If in the midst of being hurt you have become bitter, angry, resentful, retaliatory, or critical, you have sinned. You can hold onto this—all the while shouting words of self-justification—and never find relief. Not only will you continue to suffer the results of bitterness, you will increase your burden with the guilt that comes whenever you cover and hide your sin. You will do nothing more than add to your pain.

Instead, you could turn to the Lord in genuine humility and cry out for His cleansing.

> *Are you willing to humbly admit your sin?*

2. EMBRACE GOD S SOVEREIGNTY

At some point you must release your rights over the situation, accept the circumstance, and embrace the fact that God has the right to do whatever He desires in your life. (I have personally found this to be the key response in overcoming harbored hurt.)

During my parents' ordeal, I became bitter. I didn't recognize its entrance—I was numb. I didn't want to read my Bible (Why should I listen to God's counsel when it didn't seem to be working?), or pray

(Why should I talk to God when He didn't seem to be listening?). I'm not proud of those thoughts, but that is honestly how I felt at the time. I was upset with God for allowing this massive hurt to come into my family's life. My words and actions began to manifest sure signs of harbored hurt.

One night I went for a walk to try to clear my mind. For many years I had often prayed a simple, sincere prayer, *"Lord, whatever You want to do to make me a man of God, that's what I want."* That night as I walked, I stopped under a big cottonwood tree. In anger and frustration, and with my fists literally clenched toward heaven, I cried aloud, "Lord, if this is what it's going to take to make me a godly man, I don't think I want it!"

The instant those words left my lips I felt ashamed, but I also knew the boil in my heart had been lanced. The truth of how I felt had erupted from my soul.

Under that tree, my gracious Father did not chide me for my honesty, but simply ministered to my heart as only He can. God lovingly and gently reminded me that He was not the author of sin. The break-up of my parents' home was not His plan, nor His fault. In fact, He reminded me, He was the only One who could take this horrible situation and "work it for good" if I would let Him. He was the Redeemer who had expressly come to lift me up and to ultimately provide a way of escape from this sin-plagued world. For the next several minutes that cottonwood tree became my private sanctuary as the Lord stooped to lovingly help one of His confused children.

What happened next is difficult to explain. For months I had been keeping my hands clenched, telling the Lord, "I will not accept this situation." (This, of course, was ridiculous because the situation was there regardless). There was nothing I could do about the presence of the hurt, but there was something I could do about its power. With God's gentle guidance, I relaxed my hands and accepted the circumstance and its purposes for my life.

That night the sting of bitterness began to leave me. Years later I came to more fully understand that under the cottonwood tree I had begun to embrace God's sovereign control over my life. If, in the economy of God, He desired to allow such a hurtful experience, then He had also promised grace to survive … and to thrive. He was big enough to bring purpose in the midst of pain.

How are your fists? Still clenched? Are you willing to believe that God is bigger than your problem and can work it out for your good and His glory?

> *Are you willing, right now, to begin to embrace God's sovereignty over your life?*

3. FORGIVE – RELEASE THE DEBT

If your bitterness has a face behind it, you will need to take the step of unconditionally forgiving the one who has offended you. There is no other way to remove the harbored hurt.

Paul tells us in I Corinthians 13:5 that genuine love "does not take into account a wrong suffered." When real love is in our hearts, we don't keep a debt of suffered wrongs. Paul uses an accounting term describing a merchant who keeps tally of what each customer owes him. He keeps these records because he fully intends to collect payment.

Many of us keep a ledger-book in our hearts. When someone hurts us, we enter their name in our ledger. We think they shouldn't have treated us as they did (and we may be right), so we hold them accountable. "They owe me," we reason, "and I will make them pay." Then we set out to exact payment.

But listen to what God has to say about this practice.

> *Never pay back evil for evil to anyone ...*
> *Never take your own revenge, beloved, but leave room for the wrath of God, for it is written, 'Vengeance is Mine, I will repay,' says the Lord ... do not be overcome by evil, but overcome evil with good. (Romans 12:17-21)*

When we are hurt, we have only two choices:

Choice #1: We can enter the hurt in our heart's ledger and plan to get revenge.

We are amazingly creative at how we collect our debts. We might withdraw from the relationship, criticize or slander the one who hurt us, erupt in anger, plot ways to hurt them or ruin their reputation, attempt to thwart their success, question their motives, ignore them, spread rumors ... Our options are endless. We can even put a mask on our revenge with a closed mouth and pious smile. If our heart is angry though, we have already murdered our enemy (Matt. 5:21-22).

The irony of record-keeping and revenge-seeking is that we end up hurting ourselves more than the one we hold liable. A vengeful attitude aborts the development of Christlike character, shackles us with chains of bitterness and anger, and can ultimately destroy our lives. Furthermore, it can cause God to "stand down" from disciplining and correcting those who hurt us. When we attempt to seek our own justice, we may obstruct God's. God does not need vigilantes.

A friend once told me, when I was tempted to seek revenge from a person who had wronged me, "Bill, God only allows two people at a time in the boxing ring. If you want to get into the ring and try to fight your own battles, God will let you. But He'll get out. If you want God to fight your battles for you, then you must get out of the ring … and stay out."

Choice 2: We can release the debt, and transfer collection rights to God.

Forgiveness is not an act of our emotions, but a choice of our will. Just as a merchant can cancel a debt from his ledger, you can erase every debt you are holding against those who have wronged you, regardless of how you feel.

Essentially, forgiveness is an act of faith. When we choose to abandon the role of judge, jury, and executioner, we are acknowledging that God is sufficient to handle those who have hurt us. We transfer all collection rights to Him. The case is no longer in our hands, but entirely in His.

If we choose this biblical path, we will never be disappointed. God is good enough, just enough, and wise enough to deal with our offender in the proper manner. He always does it right! We seldom do.

To your amazement, you may discover God's name recorded in your ledger. Are you angry with Him over some injustice done to you? A good indicator would be to check your proximity to Him. Have you withdrawn from His fellowship? If so, it may be because you have wrongly concluded that He is not to be trusted. God could have prevented the hurt from coming your way, but for whatever reason He did not. Now He may be the one toward whom your bitterness is aimed. As you release your debts, you must fully repent of what you are holding in your heart against God.

As you review the ledger-book in your heart, what names are entered there? Perhaps there is one that appears many times, with several documented offenses. Their debt to you is great. How long do you plan to hold them in contempt? Until they die?

Until you die?

What must someone do, what price must they pay, in order to be restored to your good graces? Or, have you already determined that whatever they do will never be enough? Full repayment cannot be achieved.

Will you, by a choice of your will and as an act of faith, release every debt in your heart?

Will you, right now, forgive?

4. ASK GOD TO FILL YOUR HEART WITH HIS PURIFYING LOVE

We are clearly commanded to love everyone, even our enemies (Matt.5:38-48). You may think this is impossible, and it would be if God were not involved. If you have come into a genuine relationship with God through faith in Christ, the Holy Spirit resides in your heart. All the love that He is dwells within you (1 Jn. 4:7-8). Therefore, if you are willing to fully surrender to Him, in addition to removing the hurt,

God can miraculously pour out His love in your heart. Love is a "fruit of the Spirit" (Gal. 5:22), and can replace the acid of bitterness with the sweetness of compassion. What an amazing and healing exchange!

Would you ask God to fill your heart with His love—particularly for the individual who hurt you? If you cooperate with God, you will discover an outpouring of His power in your life. You may find yourself looking and acting very much like the Christ who lives within you!

> *Would you, right now,*
> *ask God to flood your heart with His love?*

5. THANK GOD FOR THE EXPERIENCE

There is a difference between "thanking God" and "being thankful." Thankfulness is an emotion that we sometimes feel and sometimes don't. We may not *feel* thankful about a situation that has come into our lives, but we are called by God to continually *give thanks* (1 Thess. 5:18; Eph. 5:20; Phil. 4:4).

Why would God make such a seemingly impossible command?

Our Great Physician knows that thanksgiving has amazing remedial properties. Giving thanks reminds us of God's might, and lifts us up to view the situation from His perspective. The obedient response of thanksgiving takes our mind off the pain and focuses our thoughts on the purposes of God.

Such faith-based thanksgiving is able to say, "Lord, even though I don't understand it, and may not feel like it, I believe You are sufficient for this situation … and I thank You. You have not left Your throne.

This did not take You by surprise. You have ample grace and sovereign purposes for me in the midst of my hurt."

Would you, as an act of faith, thank God for what He can and will do through this painful experience?

6. KEEP CONTINUALLY AND INSTANTLY FORGIVING

Don't think for a moment that your enemy, the devil, will take defeat lying down. You may encounter a multitude of additional opportunities to exercise faith and forgiveness—sometimes involving the same person. Satan may even parade the past hurt through your memory and try to revive your former emotions of anger and revenge.

When this happens, you could choose to relive the situation and pick up the hurt of the past. Or, you could realize that God is developing you into a godly man or woman, and that your character is strengthened by every act of the common day. Each hurt that comes your way is a fresh opportunity to forgive and love like He forgives and loves (Eph. 4:32).

The continued presence of difficulty is an indication that God has not given up on teaching you how to be like Him. And if you have any desire to be like God, you must learn to forgive.

Will you continue to forgive?

About a year after my father left home, we began to notice some unusual behavior in my mother. A series of tests revealed that she had Alzheimer's disease, and we were told that it was progressing rapidly.

As Mother deteriorated, we moved her from her home to a nearby apartment. My sister and her family, and my wife and I, then had the privilege of taking care of Mother. Although difficult, it was an honor to give some return to this one who had given so much to us.

One day I went into Mother's room and found her in a semi-conscious state. I picked her up in my arms and literally carried her to the car, then rushed her to the local hospital. There the doctor informed us that Mother had suffered a cerebral hemorrhage. That afternoon she slipped into a coma, and we were told that she might not live through the weekend. Both my brothers were away—one living in another town and the other on a preaching mission in Romania. For several days I tried unsuccessfully to reach my brother in Romania. I finally told the Lord He would have to get in touch with him because there was no way I could. About three hours later he phoned. When I asked him how he knew to call, he explained that he had felt deeply impressed to contact us. I told him that

Mother was dying, and that if he wanted to see her he needed to come as soon as possible.

After a week in a coma, Mother woke up. My brothers and their wives were scheduled to arrive the next day. My sister and I strained to understand Mother as she tried to talk, but it was very difficult. Only one word was clear to us, and Mother repeated this word at least three times …

"Forgive," she said.

We were overwhelmed. We didn't know if she was telling us to be sure and tell Dad one more time that she had forgiven him, or if she was reminding us to continue to forgive him. We finally decided to let the Holy Spirit apply this to each of our hearts as He desired.

The next day our family gathered around my mother's bed. She was awake and able to hear. For three hours we experienced the greatest worship service I may ever know this side of heaven. We sang and prayed, read Scripture, reminisced, and laughed and cried. We thanked Mother for her tremendous sacrifices and the manifold investments she had made in our lives. God gave us a precious time around her bedside … and the best was yet to happen.

The phone rang. We stood in stunned silence when we realized the call was from my dad. Although all of us had talked to Dad at times, and had taken every biblical step we knew to help bring him to repentance, it had been over two years since he had talked to Mother. But when we put the phone to her ear, her face lit up with joy. Tears streamed down her cheeks as she tried to voice words of forgiveness and love. Dad expressed his great sorrow and repentance, and asked Mother if she could find it in her heart to forgive him.

After my brother spoke briefly to Dad, he relayed the whole conversation to all of us. There was silence … and then waves of great joy and thanksgiving as God filled that hospital room with His grace and healing. It was a holy moment.

The next morning when I entered the room, Mother was talking! She said, "Billy, isn't it great about Dad calling! Why, this is what we've been praying for, that he would return to the Lord!"

Later that night, Mother slipped into a coma again. To the amazement of all, she lived another five weeks. We often wondered why God allowed her to linger, but later realized that someone had heard about Christ in that hospital room almost every day. God's delay in delivering Mother physically was, in reality, His design for delivering others spiritually.

Our entire family was able to gather one last time around Mother's bed just a few days before she died. This time there was something very different … Dad was with us. God had given us back our father! The grace God had given my mother to forgive had paved the way for him to repent and return. Since that day, my father's repentance has been abundant and clear, and he has granted me permission to tell his story, hoping it might spare others from making similar destructive choices. He and his wife have been fully restored to fellowship with all of us, and God has once again used my father to minister in the lives of many.

My mother loved poetry. During the last two years of her life she often recited the following verse:

He drew a circle and shut us out;
Daunting rebel, a thing to flout.
But love and I had a whit to win;
We drew a circle and brought him in.

In the early days of this ordeal, my mother had an encounter with the Lord that shaped her future responses. In fact, she often mentioned it to me as one of those watershed moments in her spiritual pilgrimage. As she wrestled to understand God's purposes, she came to a point of surrender where she told the Lord, "All I want, Father, is for You to receive glory."

Mother knew she would never be remarried to her husband. She knew her life would never be the same. She realized the road ahead would be filled with suffering, but she also knew a God Who had walked with her throughout her life and had prepared her for an eternity beyond.

Her settled surrender to a higher purpose determined the course for her days and opened the door for God to use her life as a testimony of forgiveness and faithfulness. (In fact, your reading this story is one more example that God has abundantly answered Mother's prayer.)

What about you? As your children and grandchildren hear the story of your life, what will they learn of God? Will they perceive a God Who is bigger than any problem or hurt … that is perfect in His dealings and redemptive in His work? Will they "taste and see that the Lord is good"?

Will they know, by God's grace through you, the incredible power of forgiveness?

OVERCOMING BITTERNESS

Many people will not actively deal with harbored hurt, even though they may recognize its presence. They simply walk away and resolve nothing. I hope you decide otherwise.

The following pages will help you personally process what you have read in this booklet. The few minutes it will take to complete this exercise could, in fact, change your life.

As you work through the "Overcoming Bitterness" exercise, I encourage you to:

- **BE HONEST.**
  You cannot hide anything from God anyway.
- **BE THOROUGH.**
  Let God go all the way to the bottom of your hurt.
- **READ THE SCRIPTURES INDICATED.**
  God can powerfully use His Word to change your mind and heal your soul.
- **PRAY.**
  Ask God to help you come to a complete resolution.

OVERCOMING

ACKNOWLEDGE YOUR HURT
PSALM 142

List the people and circumstances that have hurt you.

ADMIT YOUR SIN
I PETER 2:19–25

List any ways you may have sinned as a result of being hurt.

BITTERNESS
(HEBREWS 12:10–17)

GAIN GOD S PERSPECTIVE ROMANS 8:18–39

List character traits which God might wish to develop in you through a right response to your hurts.

CHOOSE GODLY RESPONSES

Have you …

confessed your sin?
(Proverbs 28:13)

☐ Yes

☐ No

cleared your conscience?
(Matthew 5:23)

☐ Yes

☐ No

thanked God?
(1 Thessalonians 5:18)

☐ Yes

☐ No

blessed your offender?
(Romans 12:17-21)

☐ Yes

☐ No

Other Writings by Bill Elliff

WhiteWater
Navigating the Rapids of Church Conflict

The Child of 10,000 Names
An illustrated Christmas allegory about the most important birth in history!

Lifting the Load
How to Gain and Maintain a Clear Conscience

Turning the Tide
Having MORE Kids who Follow Christ
(Holly Elliff with Bill Elliff)

Everyman
the Rescue

50 Marks of a Man of God
Important questions for those in spiritual leadership

Personal Revival Checklist
A spiritual examinat
from the Sermon on the Mount.

To order resources, contact TruthInkPublications.com.

Bulk prices available upon request.